MINI MECHANICS

DIGGERS AND DUMPERS

make believe ideas

MINI MECHANICS

Welcome to our **workshop.** Meet the **crew!** We've got some awesomely **tough vehicles** in today. Come and have a look!

Hi, I'm **Nelson Nut**!

Hi, I'm **Jenson Jack**, and I'm the boss!

  Remember: you must never play around vehicles, and tools are NOT toys!

TOOLS

A good **mechanic** needs great tools and equipment. Take a look in our **toolbox** and find out about our favorites!

Pliers can grip parts that are too tiny for fingers!

Jacks lift vehicles up so we can look underneath them.

Nuts and bolts are used to hold two or more parts together.

jack

nuts and bolts

Wrenches are used to tighten and loosen nuts

BULLDOZER

Bulldozers are incredibly **strong**, just like real **bulls!** You'll find bulldozers on **construction sites** or anywhere **earth, rocks, trees,** or even **buildings** need to be dug up, knocked down, or pushed away!

blade

Curved **blades** carry loads, and straight blades push things away.

The world's biggest bulldozer, built by

GRADER

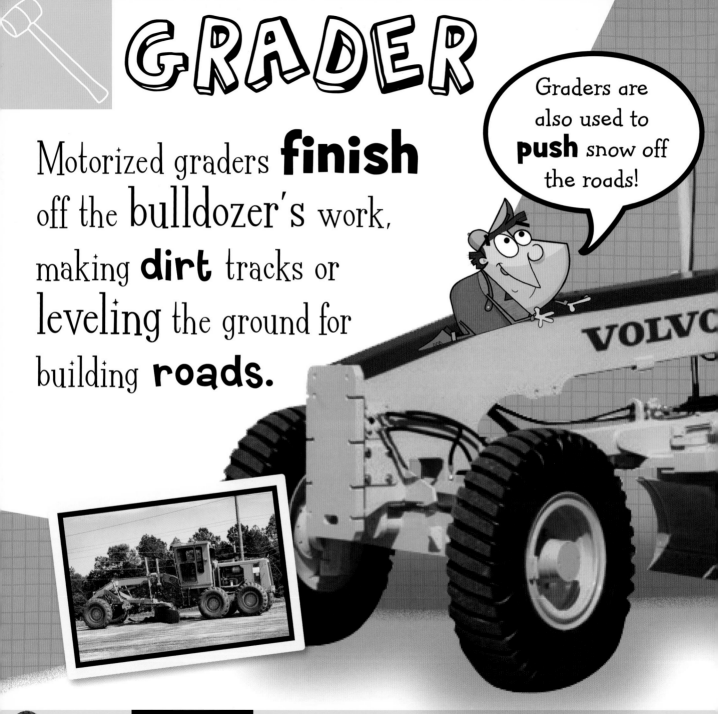

Motorized graders **finish** off the bulldozer's work, making **dirt** tracks or leveling the ground for building **roads.**

Graders are also used to **push** snow off the roads!

This mighty grader is 30 ft (9 m) long and weighs

light

cab

exhaust

The super-strong **blade** scrapes the ground to make it flat.

blade

EXCAVATOR

The excavator's main job is to **dig**. On building sites, excavators dig **holes** for **foundations**, but you'll also find them in **mines** and on **demolition sites**.

cab

house

The **cab** can turn in a full circle thanks to a giant **pin** that connects the **house** and **undercarriage**.

undercarriage...

The world's biggest excavator, the Bagger 293,

DUMP TRUCK

Dump trucks are super-strong **load-carriers.** You see them on the **road,** carrying **gravel** or **sand** to building sites.

This truck has three rows of **wheels.** The biggest dumpers have seven rows!

wheel .....

The Liebherr T282 is one of the biggest dump trucks

Stickers to use on the activity pages.

Extras to stick where you want.

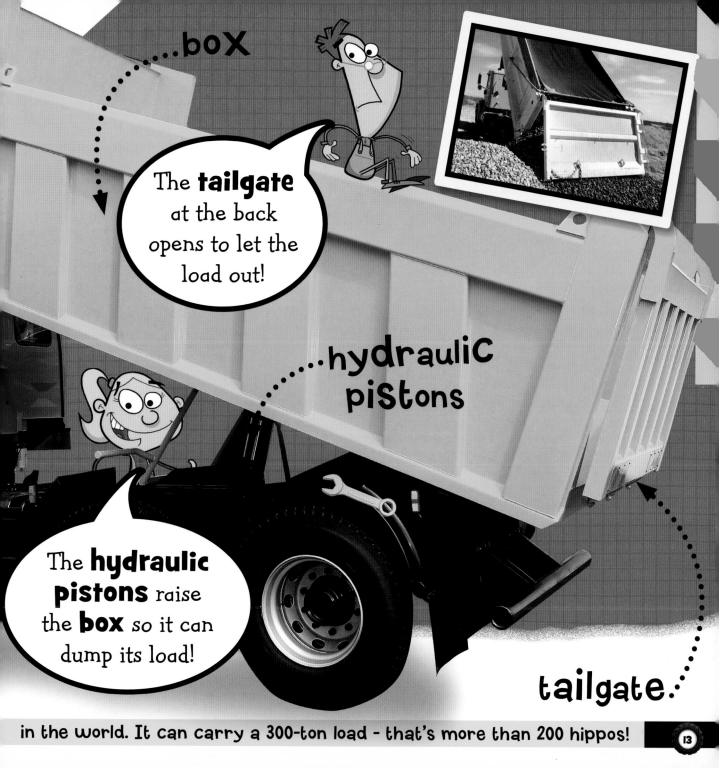

box

The **tailgate** at the back opens to let the load out!

hydraulic pistons

The **hydraulic pistons** raise the **box** so it can dump its load!

tailgate

in the world. It can carry a 300-ton load - that's more than 200 hippos!

BACKHOE LOADER

Backhoe loaders are **tractors** with special **attachments!** They are **great** for small jobs like mending **roads** or digging **ditches.**

backhoe

This is the **backhoe**. It's like a mini-excavator!

cab

The **seat** turns around so the driver can face the front or back!

The **shovel** moves and scoops things just like a mini-bulldozer!

shovel

This mini-marvel can lift nearly three tons or the weight of 150 children!

WHEEL LOADER

> The massive **bucket** scoops up its load and carries it away!

Wheel loaders are hardworking **machines** that can be seen on construction sites, carrying **earth** and **rubble** to **load** onto trucks.

...bucket

The largest loader in the world is LeTourneau

Great job! Now take the quiz to earn your
Mini Mechanics Gold Award!

Find stickers to complete the report.

This vehicle's clawlike ripper breaks up land or rock into small pieces.

The hydraulic pistons raise the box so it can dump its load!

The shovel moves and scoops things just like a mini-bulldozer!

The massive bucket scoops things up and carries them away.

MINI MECHANICS
GOLD AWARD CERTIFICATE

This is to certify that .... has achieved the

Mini Mechanics Gold Award

for excellence in

Diggers and dumpers

Good job!

Sticker a star here!